Where Is Alcatraz?

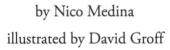

by Nico Medina

illustrated by David Groff

Grosset & Dunlap
An Imprint of Penguin Random House

To Jane O'Connor—for letting me nerd out!—NM

To Jimmy Lutz, a great friend—DG

GROSSET & DUNLAP
Penguin Young Readers Group
An Imprint of Penguin Random House

Text copyright © 2016 by Nicolas Medina. Illustrations copyright © 2016 by Penguin Random House LLC. All rights reserved. Published by Grosset & Dunlap, an imprint of Penguin Random House LLC, 345 Hudson Street, New York, New York 10014. Who HQ™ and all related logos are trademarks owned by Penguin Random House LLC. GROSSET & DUNLAP is a trademark of Penguin Random House LLC. Printed in the USA.

Library of Congress Cataloging-in-Publication Data is available.

ISBN 9780448488837 (paperback)   10 9 8 7 6 5 4 3 2 1
ISBN 9780399542329 (library binding)   10 9 8 7 6 5 4 3 2 1

Contents

Where Is Alcatraz?

On a cool and foggy day in San Francisco, California, hundreds of people are waiting to board a large ferryboat. They bought their tickets days, weeks, even *months* in advance.

Young and old have come here from all across the United States. Some have traveled from Japan, Brazil, and India. All these people are at Pier 33 in San Francisco for one reason: to go to prison!

But not just any prison. They are here to see Alcatraz, the most famous prison in American history.

Today, Alcatraz Island—also known as "The Rock"—is a national park visited by more than a million people every year. It is reached by boat, one and a half miles across from San Francisco. The violent criminals who once called The Rock home—men like Al "Scarface" Capone and George "Machine Gun" Kelly—no longer live there. Nowadays the island's residents are mostly nesting seabirds.

However, the prison that held criminals for nearly three decades still stands. Years of pounding waves and stiff sea breezes have eroded its walls, causing the buildings to slowly crumble. But the legends of Alcatraz—tales of evil spirits, dark dungeons, and bold escape attempts—live on to this day.

CHAPTER 1
Island of the Pelicans

The first human visitors to Alcatraz Island were probably Native Americans. They may have rowed their canoes there to fish and collect eggs from seabirds' nests. But they wouldn't live on the island. They may have used it as a place to banish people. They believed evil spirits haunted the island.

Juan Manuel de Ayala

Alcatraz Island, in foggy San Francisco Bay, remained hidden from Spanish explorers for more than two centuries. In 1775, a young Spanish naval officer named Juan Manuel de Ayala was the first to spot The Rock, which was covered in pelicans. He named the steep, barren island Isla de los Alcatraces—or "Island of the Pelicans" in Spanish.

On June 29, 1776, Spanish colonists founded a mission, or church, on the mainland. They named the mission after Saint Francis of Assisi— or "San Francisco" in Spanish.

When Mexico won its independence from Spain in 1821, San Francisco and the rest of California became part of Mexico. In 1846, the United States and Mexico began a bloody war over land in the West. The United States took over California after the Mexican-American War ended in 1848. That same year, gold was discovered in California!

San Francisco

THE UNITED STATES

MEXICO

The Western
United States in:

1845

1848

1853

San Francisco was a
small town until the Gold
Rush. As people moved west
in search of gold, the city's
population exploded, from
a few hundred in 1848 to
over thirty thousand just
one year later.

San Francisco quickly
became America's biggest
and most important city
on the West Coast. America
needed to defend it against its enemies.

Alcatraz Island, standing guard over San
Francisco in the middle of the bay, was the perfect
place for a fortress.

Work began on Fort Alcatraz in 1853. One
man said the island was nothing but solid rock
covered by a tiny bit of soil, with a "crust" of bird
poop on top! The sandstone on Alcatraz could be

cut with a hatchet. So stronger building materials had to be shipped in from as far away as New York City and China.

A lighthouse opened in 1854. It was the first one on the West Coast of the United States. By December 1859, construction of the citadel, or fortress, was complete. The three-story citadel stood on the island's highest point. The citadel's brick walls were more than four feet thick and had many narrow slits from which to fire rifles.

Eventually, Fort Alcatraz held more than one hundred cannons, which could shoot four-hundred-pound cannonballs a distance of nearly three miles! Later, when the citadel became housing for officers, these cannonballs were used to decorate the gardens!

The United States during the Civil War

Union states
Border states (part of the Union)
Confederate states
Territories
West Virginia
(separated from Virginia in 1861 and joined the Union in 1865)

Brigadier General
Edwin Sumner

In 1861, Fort Alcatraz was put on high alert. The states of the American South had split from the Union. They formed a new country called the Confederate States of America. The Civil War had begun.

Brigadier General Edwin Sumner, the man in charge of Fort Alcatraz, told his soldiers to fire upon any ship that was flying a Confederate flag. Alcatraz not only defended San Francisco from Confederate attack, it also became a military prison. Soldiers who left their posts or committed crimes were sent to the island to serve their time. The crew of a Confederate ship was also imprisoned at Alcatraz.

Life on The Rock was terrible. Prisoners were forced to do hard labor all day. As many as fifteen men lived in just one dark basement cell. To make matters worse, there was no heat. And no toilets—only buckets!

Prisoners constructing Alcatraz

Over the coming years, more cells were built on Alcatraz—mostly by the prisoners themselves. By 1904, there was room for more than three hundred prisoners on the island. Most of the prisoners on Alcatraz were serving short sentences. But some were in for more serious crimes, like murder.

Conditions at Alcatraz improved for the prisoners. They only stayed in their cells to sleep. During the day, the men had jobs to do. Some built roads or cleaned the prison. Those who could not read or write went to school, while others learned trades, like bookbinding. When they weren't working, some prisoners were allowed to walk freely around the island. Some even worked as servants for families of officers living on the island—or even as babysitters!

One group was regularly taken to nearby Angel Island, where they kept vegetable gardens. And in the 1920s, some prisoners fought in boxing matches that were held in San Francisco. Local businesses even sold tickets to the events!

Security was not tight. This led to a number of men trying to escape Alcatraz—by stealing rowboats or by swimming. But swimming in the frigid, choppy waters of the bay ended either in drowning or turning around to be rescued.

The San Francisco Earthquake of 1906

By 1906, San Francisco had grown into a major city of four hundred thousand people. Its famous cable cars—still in use today—took people up and down busy city streets. But in the early morning hours of April 18, a massive earthquake shook the city for nearly a minute. The earthquake was so big, it was felt by people as far away as Oregon, Los Angeles, and Nevada.

San Francisco was ruined. Fires raged for three days, destroying almost five hundred city blocks.

More than three thousand people lost their lives, and half the city's residents suddenly became homeless. They pitched tents in parks and cooked their food in the streets.

Though there wasn't much damage on Alcatraz, San Francisco's other jails did not escape the earthquake. When fires approached the jails, the inmates had to be moved. So Alcatraz opened its cell doors (and then locked them!) to 176 civilian (meaning nonmilitary) prisoners from the city, until the city jails could house them again.

Around 1909, construction began on an even larger cell house. This giant concrete building would have enough space for six hundred prisoners in individual cells. The cell house would also contain an auditorium, a library, a shower room, a hospital, a kitchen, and a dining room. It was a huge project, and it took the prisoners three years to build! The building still stands today, more than a century later.

The library at Alcatraz

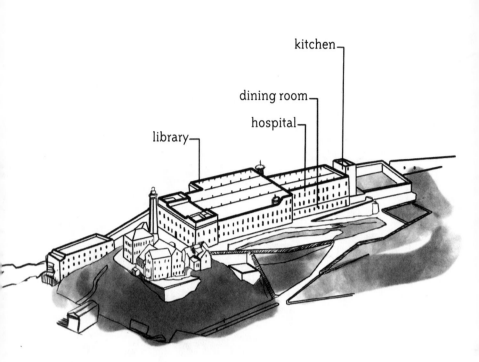

kitchen

dining room

hospital

library

But soon, the US military decided it was too expensive to keep Alcatraz open. In 1934, The Rock was handed over to the US Department of Justice (DOJ).

Violent crime was on the rise in America. The crooks of the day were bold and fearless. They robbed banks at gunpoint. They kidnapped rich men and women for ransom money. Mobsters killed one another in city streets. More people were being sent to prison than ever before.

The DOJ had plans for Alcatraz—plans that *didn't* include gardening trips to Angel Island or babysitting gigs.

Alcatraz would become US Penitentiary Alcatraz: a maximum-security prison big enough, strict enough, and tough enough to lock up America's worst criminals. And it would serve as a warning to would-be crooks: Watch out, or you'll get shipped to Alcatraz.

Perhaps most important of all: The Rock would be "escape-proof."

CHAPTER 2
Gangland

Crime rose in America in the 1920s and 1930s for two major reasons: the Great Depression and Prohibition.

The Great Depression lasted from 1929 to 1939. It was the worst economic crisis in American history. Many of the country's banks failed. Millions lost their jobs, their homes, and their savings. In 1933, the worst year of the Depression, one out of every four American workers didn't have a job. Sometimes when people become desperate for money, they turn to crime.

Prohibition also led to more crime. It made selling, making, and shipping alcoholic beverages illegal in America. Prohibition was the law of the land from 1920 to 1933. But many Americans still bought liquor illegally.

Gangs of organized criminals—known as the mob—controlled much of the buying and selling of illegal alcohol. The mob had been around in America since the late 1800s. It was an organized crime ring that operated in big cities across the country.

Barrels of illegal liquor

One of the most successful mobsters of the day—who would later become Alcatraz's most famous inmate—was a man named Al "Scarface" Capone.

Al Capone

Alphonse Capone was born in Brooklyn, New York, on January 17, 1899. He was one of nine children. His parents had left southern Italy for America just five years earlier. The family lived in an apartment down the street from Al's father's barbershop.

Al was a smart boy. But downtown Brooklyn was an easy place to find trouble. It didn't take Al long to fall in with the wrong crowd. At fourteen, he dropped out of school and joined a gang of tough street kids.

Around this time, Al met an older man named Johnny Torrio. Johnny was an important New York City crime boss. He took Al under his wing. Johnny showed Al that it was important to lead a quiet life at home, even if he made money through crime.

For a while, though, Al held down legal jobs. He

Johnny Torrio

worked at a bookbinding factory and a bowling alley. After Al got married in 1918, he worked as an accountant, handling money for a construction company. People in the neighborhood knew Al Capone to be a good man and a leader.

Then Johnny Torrio introduced Al to Frankie Yale. He was a gangster who owned a bar in Brooklyn. Al soon joined Frankie's gang. Frankie was a different kind of teacher. Unlike Johnny, Frankie Yale taught Al about using violence to get what you wanted.

Frankie Yale

When Al got into a fight at Frankie's bar one night, his left cheek was slashed with a knife or razor blade. That's what gave him his nickname: "Scarface."

Meanwhile, Johnny Torrio moved to Chicago. When Prohibition became law in 1920, he started bringing liquor in from Canada and selling it in the States. This was called *bootlegging*. Soon Johnny invited Al to move to Chicago and help him run things. And Al said yes.

By the mid-1920s, the liquor was flowing freely in the Windy City. More than a thousand gangs ruled Chicago's streets. It was a violent and bloody time. After someone tried to kill Johnny Torrio, he decided to move to Italy for a while.

That left Al to run the business. Money poured into his pockets. By 1929, Al Capone was bringing in more than $60 million annually. (That's worth more than $830 million today!)

Al made friends with cops and City Hall

politicians, then paid them money not to arrest him. Bootleggers competing with Al were either paid to give up their business, or killed. In Chicago, people who liked their liquor *loved* Al Capone.

One man who *didn't* love Al Capone was George "Bugs" Moran. Bugs was a rival gang member. He wanted a piece of Al's business, and he had tried to kill Al and Johnny Torrio before. It is believed that Al Capone ordered Jack McGurn, one of his hit men, to kill Bugs.

Jack cooked up a nasty scheme. On Valentine's Day 1929, Jack lured Bugs Moran's gang to a garage to buy some cheap liquor.

Bugs Moran

Jack and his men showed up at the garage dressed as cops. They told Bugs's gang to face the wall. Bugs's gang thought they were under arrest. But when they turned around, Capone's men took out their machine guns and opened fire, killing all seven men. This bloody event came to be known as the Saint Valentine's Day Massacre.

Bugs Moran survived—he had never gone inside the garage.

Al was more than a thousand miles away, at his home in Miami Beach, Florida. That was the plan. Now he couldn't be accused of killing anyone.

But the Saint Valentine's Day Massacre turned the public against Capone. He was named "Public Enemy Number One" by the Chicago Crime Commission, a group of concerned citizens who thought he was the worst gangster in Chicago. It took until 1931, but Al Capone was finally charged with a crime—*failing to pay his taxes*! He was found guilty, and sentenced to eleven years in prison.

Al Capone served two years at the federal prison in Atlanta, Georgia. Federal prisons are for criminals who have committed a federal crime.

Federal crimes are ones that break laws passed by the federal government, rather than laws passed by the states. These crimes include airplane hijacking, bank robbery, and tax evasion.

Capone led a comfortable life in his Atlanta prison cell. He had a nice desk, a comfortable armchair, special bedsheets, and a rug. He hid cash in his cell, which he used to bribe prison guards. Sometimes Al and the guards listened to the radio together. Al's family and friends moved to a nearby hotel, so he could have visitors every day.

But on August 18, 1934, Al Capone was removed from his cell. He was handcuffed, shackled, and put on a train with fifty-two other inmates.

For days, the train chugged across the country. Al Capone was on his way to Alcatraz. Finally, the train reached San Francisco. Normally, a boat would have taken prisoners across the bay, to The Rock.

But the warden—the man in charge of Alcatraz—wasn't taking any chances that Capone would try to escape from the train. So what did he do? He had the entire train car loaded onto a barge, which was towed across the choppy waters to the island prison.

The Warden's Mansion

The warden lived in a three-story, seventeen-room mansion on Alcatraz. The house offered beautiful views of San Francisco and—after it opened in 1937—the famous Golden Gate Bridge. The mansion also featured lush gardens and a greenhouse, which were cared for by an inmate. Most of the mansion burned in 1970, but its remains can still be seen today.

Besides the warden's mansion and the cell house on Alcatraz, there were other buildings. The Model Industries Building—and later, the New Industries Building—was where inmates went to work to build things. Alcatraz even had its own power plant to generate electricity!

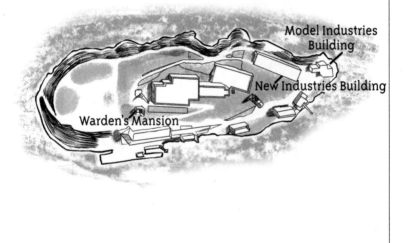

Model Industries Building

New Industries Building

Warden's Mansion

Alcatraz had been a federal prison for less than a year. Now it became home to the most famous gangster in the country. Al Capone, Public Enemy Number One, was now known simply as #85-AZ, Alcatraz's eighty-fifth civilian prisoner.

Warden James A. Johnston made the rules here. And according to the warden, Alcatraz was

U. S. PENITENTIARY
ALCATRAZ
85

"minimum privilege, maximum security."

Here on The Rock, there would be:

No talking.

One visitor per month.

And absolutely *no* bribery.

Al once said: "It looks like Alcatraz has got me licked."

Other Famous Alcatraz Inmates

George "Machine Gun" Kelly was nicknamed for his favorite weapon, the Thompson submachine gun. His first was a gift from his wife. A bank robber, bootlegger, and kidnapper, he was caught in 1933 after kidnapping a wealthy oilman.

George "Machine Gun" Kelly

Alvin "Creepy" Karpis was called "Creepy" because of his evil-looking grin. He teamed up with brothers Fred and "Doc" Barker—and their mother,

"Ma" Barker—to form a gang that became famous for deadly bank robberies. Creepy Karpis was captured and served longer than any other man at Alcatraz—almost twenty-six years.

Robert Stroud, known as the "Birdman of Alcatraz," raised and studied hundreds of birds while imprisoned in Kansas. He even published a book called *The Diseases of Canaries* in 1933. He was moved to Alcatraz in 1942, but he had to leave his birds behind.

Robert Stroud

Alvin "Creepy" Karpis

CHAPTER 3
Welcome to The Rock

Alcatraz opened for business as a federal prison in July 1934. After a boat arrived, men were unloaded onto the dock. Here, armed guards lined them up and then marched them, still cuffed and shackled, up a long hill toward the cell house.

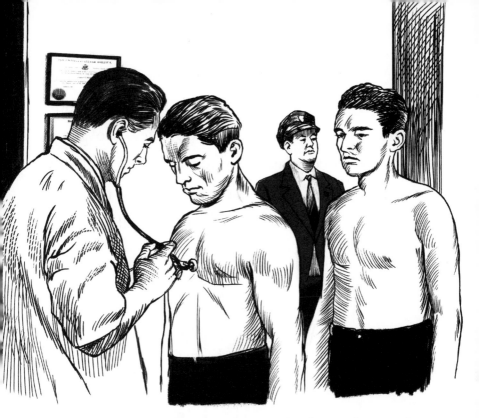

Families of the officers who worked on The Rock watched from their apartment windows, which overlooked the dock.

When the prisoners arrived at the cell house, they were led into the basement. Their cuffs and leg irons were removed. They were each photographed and given an inmate number. Then there was a medical exam.

After showering, the new inmates received their uniform: blue button-up shirt, blue-and-white pants, belt, socks, shoes. They also got a cap, a wool coat, and a raincoat, for the cold and wet days ahead. Carrying their clothes, the men were now taken, still naked, to their cells.

Each inmate had his own cell. This small living space measured nine feet long by five feet wide. The ceiling was seven feet high. There was room for only a single cot, a small worktable, shelf, toilet, and sink. The mattress was just five inches thick.

But the men would have to get used to it. They spent at least fourteen hours a day in their cells. Inmates who didn't get jobs, however, could expect to be in the cells twenty-three hours a day.

Cell House Tour

The cell house at Alcatraz contained four blocks of cells. Each cellblock contained two rows and three levels of cells.

Long corridors separated the cellblocks. The inmates nicknamed some of these walkways after famous streets and landmarks in New York City. "Broadway," which separated B Block from C Block, led to "Times Square," where a clock hung on the wall above the dining-hall entrance. "Seedy Street" (or "C-D") separated C Block from D Block. Seedy Street ended at a doorway that opened onto the Yard.

A library that contained more than ten thousand books and magazines sat in the corner of the cell house. Its high ceilings let in lots of sunlight. The row of cells with a view of the library was considered the nicest in Alcatraz. Their "address" was "Park Avenue."

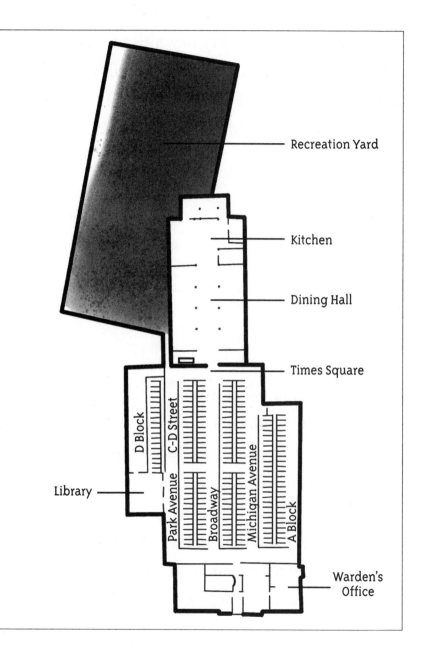

Recreation Yard

Kitchen

Dining Hall

Times Square

D Block

C–D Street

Park Avenue

Broadway

Michigan Avenue

A Block

Library

Warden's Office

A booklet awaited every new prisoner in their cells. It listed all the rules—everything from when to wake up, eat, and work, to the number of library books you could keep in your cell.

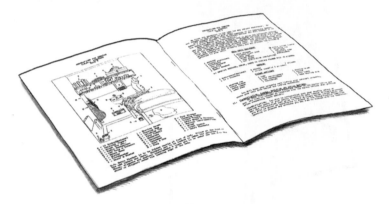

The rules were to be followed to the letter, or the inmate would be punished.

The worst troublemakers were sent to the Dungeons. That was the nickname given to the cold, damp, pitch-black cells beneath A and D Blocks.

The Dungeons had no pillows, bedding, sinks, or toilets. A Dungeon inmate ate a diet of mostly bread and water. He slept on the cold cement

floor. There were stories of men who had to stand, handcuffed to the bars, for hours on end.

Warden Johnston shut down the Dungeons in 1938. From then on, D Block became the new cellblock for extra punishment, such as solitary confinement. (That is when prisoners are kept alone, away from other prisoners.) Men sent to D Block to do time "in solitary" couldn't eat with the rest of the prisoners. Their meals were brought to them. They were allowed just one visit to the Yard and two showers per week. The rest of their time was spent in a cell.

The best views of San Francisco could be seen from D Block. Some considered this an extra form of punishment. It showed them what they were missing. Sometimes the prisoners could hear laughter coming from the sightseeing boats that sailed past the island.

Five cells on the first floor of D Block—known as the "Hole"—could be used for even more serious punishment. The cells in the Hole had two doors: The first was made of bars, and the second was solid steel. When the steel door was shut, the Hole was plunged into total darkness.

There was a sink and toilet, and a single, dim lightbulb that could be turned on only by the guards. There was a thin mattress to sleep on, but it was taken away during the day. Inmates usually got locked up in the Hole for a day or two. But if they misbehaved, they could be held for up to nineteen days straight.

The "Strip Cell" was the worst—and most feared—form of punishment. Inmates were kept naked for up to two days at a time. Unlike the cells in the Hole, this cell had no lightbulb, toilet, or sink. To relieve himself, the prisoner used a hole in the ground.

Inmates feared the Hole and the Strip Cell. Sitting cold and alone in the dark for days was a terrifying punishment. It messed with people's minds.

The best way to avoid doing time in D Block was to always follow the rules.

Haunted Alcatraz

To this day, some people believe that the ghosts of former prisoners haunt Alcatraz. Some night watchmen say they hear slamming doors and footsteps. But they never see anyone. Once, while giving a tour of the prison, Warden Johnston was said to have heard sobbing from inside the Dungeon walls. But no one was in there.

Cell 14-D, in the infamous Hole, is said to be always

colder than the other D Block cells, even when the weather is warm. Stories have been told of a prisoner locked in 14-D who screamed all night long. He said that a creature with glowing red eyes was trying to kill him. The next morning, he was found dead.

Most people working at Alcatraz today insist there is no such thing as ghosts at Alcatraz. All these bizarre incidents, they say, have a logical explanation, or are just stories made up to scare people. But still, the legends remain.

CHAPTER 4
The Daily Grind

The men in Alcatraz were the federal prison system's biggest troublemakers. Like Al Capone, they had bribed guards. Some had attempted to escape from other prisons. (Some *actually* escaped . . . only to get caught again.) They were sent to The Rock to be "set straight"—to learn the rules, and to follow them.

Inmates were on a schedule, which was planned out to the minute. While the schedule changed a bit over the years, it never varied in its strictness. According to the 1956 rulebook, every weekday, the inmates had to rise at 7:00 on the dot. They had to get dressed and make their beds and make sure their cells were neat and tidy.

At 7:20, the inmates stood at their cell doors, while the guards counted them. Security was extremely tight at Alcatraz. The guards counted the prisoners eleven more times each day. Sometimes there were extra counts. Guards dragged their nightsticks along the bars. They were listening for hollow spots where the iron wasn't strong enough.

Inmates had to be quiet during counts. For the first few years Alcatraz was a federal prison, Warden Johnston had a "rule of silence." Inmates weren't allowed to speak to one another, except at mealtimes . . . *quietly*. This rule was eventually changed.

By 7:30, it was chow time. When their row was called, the men walked silently, single file, to the Mess Hall, where breakfast was served to all the inmates at once. While Alcatraz had room for many additional prisoners, there were rarely more than three hundred at a time. But that's still a lot of men to guard at once.

And the Mess Hall could be a dangerous place. Riots broke out a few times a year. Often they started because of the meals. Food and water had to be delivered to Alcatraz by boat. Sometimes when the kitchen went over budget, or because of food rationing during World War II, prisoners got the same cheap meal for days in a row.

When prisoners rioted, they threw food. They flipped tables and benches. They threatened guards. Forks and knives, steak bones, and even hot coffee became weapons.

Officers on the outdoor catwalk overlooking the Mess Hall would order them to stand down. If things got even worse, fourteen tear-gas canisters in the ceiling could be set off by remote control. That's why the inmates sometimes called the Mess Hall the "Gas Chamber."

Food at Alcatraz

Despite Mess Hall riots, most people thought the food on Alcatraz was the best in the federal prison system. Guards and officers ate the same food the inmates did. Meals usually changed every day and included a soup, salad, or vegetable; a starch, like potatoes; meat; and a dessert. Special meals were served on holidays, and sometimes there was live music.

After breakfast, inmates returned to their cells. If they were lucky enough to have a job, they would change into their work clothes and report for duty. Prisoners who didn't have jobs had to stay locked in their cells until lunchtime.

Some jobs on Alcatraz paid the prisoners a small hourly wage. Other jobs reduced their sentences. That meant the more an inmate worked at his job, the less time he had to serve on The Rock. On average, for every month they worked, inmates had their sentence reduced by two days.

Warden Johnston believed in the importance of work and routine. He wanted to *rehabilitate* his prisoners. That meant he wanted them to leave Alcatraz better than when they came in, and be less likely to commit more crimes.

But inmates had to earn the right to work. According to Regulation 5 in the Alcatraz rulebook, inmates were "entitled to food, clothing, shelter, and medical attention. Anything else" was "a privilege." They had to show they deserved it.

Having a job was definitely a privilege—it was a way to pass the time, to feel a little more normal. It also gave inmates the chance to learn new skills they could use after they left Alcatraz.

Over the years, the prisoners of Alcatraz made gloves, brushes, brooms, office furniture, military uniforms, and rubber mats. They also did laundry for the military bases in the area. During World War II, they made buoys to hold nets that were dropped in San Francisco Bay to help protect the city from enemy submarines!

Kitchen duty was considered one of the best jobs on Alcatraz. The hours were long, but the inmates could eat almost whenever they wanted! For everyone else, supper was served at 4:40. By 5:30, all inmates returned to their cells. For the next four hours, they could kick back and relax.

Some painted pictures or read books from the library. They couldn't browse the shelves themselves. Books were brought to them on a rolling cart. Newspapers were not allowed.

Others wrote letters. They were allowed to send two—and receive seven—every week. Each letter coming into and going out of Alcatraz was read by officers and censored. That meant anything the prisoner should not see or send was blacked out.

Visiting Hours

Inmates were allowed just one visitor per month. It could be his wife or a blood relative (no one else), and the warden had to approve the visit ahead of time.

Visits lasted only two hours. Inmates spoke to their loved ones through bulletproof glass two inches thick. They were not allowed to discuss the inmate's crime or current events in the outside world. They could not even discuss Alcatraz or its rules.

Inmates could also play stringed instruments, like guitars, in their cells until 7:00. (But singing or whistling was not allowed!) There was an orchestra room where other instruments, like pianos and drums, could be played on the weekends. Al Capone played the banjo with the Rock Islanders, the Alcatraz band.

In 1955, radio jacks were installed in each inmate's cell. From 6:00 to 9:30, prisoners could plug in their headphones and quietly listen to radio programs. On October 4, everyone was given the day off to tune into the World Series, when the Brooklyn Dodgers beat their rivals, the New York Yankees.

At 9:30, it was lights-out. Inmates were told to sleep with their pillows on the bars-side of the mattress. There would be three counts during the night.

Kids on Alcatraz

Guards and officers had lived on The Rock with their families since Alcatraz's days as a military prison. Most of them lived in a three-story apartment building that overlooked the dock. Not counting the inmates, about three hundred people at a time lived on Alcatraz.

People who grew up on Alcatraz say it was like living in a small town. There was a market and general store and a tiny post office. The Officers' Club had a gym, a dance floor, a bowling alley, and a soda fountain. There was even a playground!

But for many kids, the whole Rock was a playground. They weren't allowed near the cell house, but they could still pretend. Instead of "cops and robbers," kids played "guards and cons" ("convict" is another word for prisoner). They made up stories about secret tunnels.

Alcatraz kids went to school in San Francisco. Their "school bus" was a boat that made trips to and from the city.

But even for guards and their families, there were rules. Folks visiting San Francisco had until 9:00 p.m. every weeknight—11:00 on weekends—to catch the last boat back, or they would be stuck in town overnight. And toy knives and guns were not allowed. Kids used sticks and bananas instead.

On weekends, inmates were allowed to sleep in . . . for an extra fifteen minutes. Church services were held on Sundays and religious holidays, for those who wished to attend. And two Sundays a month, movies were shown in the auditorium.

Saturdays and Sundays, inmates got a maximum of five hours in the Yard. For most inmates, this was the highlight of the week.

They played softball and handball. They smoked cigarettes and chatted on the steps. Sometimes fights broke out. Armed guards patrolled the scene from the twenty-foot walls that surrounded the Yard.

Playing bridge and dominoes were also popular activities in the Yard. Still, this free time was not enough to satisfy some inmates. Life in prison was unbearable.

They wanted nothing short of freedom.

CHAPTER 5
Escape from Alcatraz

For some desperate prisoners, no price was too high to pay for the sweet taste of freedom. Over the course of many months in 1946, Bernie Coy (Inmate #415) came up with an escape plan that became known as the Battle of Alcatraz.

Coy worked in the library. He could move around the cell house and talk quietly with other inmates while he delivered books. Coy watched the guards carefully, learning their habits.

At Alcatraz there were strict rules for the guards as well as the prisoners.

Bernie Coy

For example, if a guard needed the key to go to the Yard, he would tap on the door. Then a guard on the West Gun Gallery—a walkway that overlooked the cell house—lowered a key to the first guard.

On the afternoon of May 2, Bernie Coy and his partners took advantage of this routine.

The cell house was mostly empty after lunch. Coy quietly swept the corridors. He tapped on the door to D Block. This was the signal for his partner "Crazy Sam" Shockley to start screaming. Crazy Sam raised a big ruckus. The officers patrolling the cell house went to D Block to see what was going on.

Meanwhile in the kitchen, inmate Marv Hubbard asked to be excused. He was finished with his work and said he wanted to go to the Yard for some fresh air. Permission was granted, and Hubbard left the kitchen. Hubbard stood outside the door, so Officer Bill Miller could search him.

At this point, Bernie Coy put down his broom and snuck up behind Officer Miller. Coy pinned Miller's arms behind his back. Then Hubbard punched the officer, knocking him out cold.

Coy took the officer's keys and opened a cell door. He had been watching for months to learn which keys opened which doors. Coy and Hubbard took Officer Miller's pants and jacket, bound and gagged him, put him in the cell, and locked him inside. Then, using Miller's keys, Coy started opening cell doors for his other friends.

Next Coy grabbed a small tool bag he had hidden. In it was a "bar-spreading" tool made from toilet fixtures. With the bag in his mouth, Coy climbed up to the Gun Gallery. He took out his tool and got to work, spreading apart the bars that protected the Gun Gallery. Coy squeezed through the tiny opening. He'd been dieting for months to be sure he'd fit through.

He found a club and crouched down to hide. He gave the signal to Joseph Cretzer, one of the men he'd just freed. Cretzer tapped on the Yard door, signaling the officer up in the Gun Gallery to come out and lower the key to him. The officer had no idea what had been happening. When he appeared, Coy hit him with the club, knocking him unconscious.

Coy quickly found a key ring and a pistol, and gave them to Cretzer. He found a rifle and took it for himself. For the next several minutes, the men tried to find the right key—#107—to open the door to the Yard. But it wasn't there. They tried all the keys. None of them worked.

Little did Coy know that Officer Miller had broken the rules earlier that day. Rather than return key #107 to the Gun Gallery that morning like he was supposed to, he had put it in his shirt pocket.

More guards and prisoners stumbled onto the scene. They were taken hostage. Coy and his men were running out of time. They demanded to know where key #107 was. Miller lied and said it must be in the Gun Gallery, where it belonged. By then Miller had hidden the key in the cell.

A guard from the basement came upstairs and realized what was happening in the cell house. He ran back downstairs and called Warden Johnston. The alarm was sounded.

Coy grabbed his rifle. He knocked out some windows and took aim, shooting at the guards in three watchtowers. Cretzer took his pistol and opened fire on the officers they had taken hostage. He wanted to leave no witnesses.

But while Cretzer wasn't looking, one of the officers wrote on the ground the names of the six prisoners who were trying to escape. Then he circled the names of the leaders: Coy, Hubbard, and Cretzer.

Officers called inside the cell house. They wanted to discuss a way to end the violence. Cretzer screamed back that he'd never be taken alive!

For three days, the Battle of Alcatraz raged on. Gunfire was exchanged. More guards were flown in from federal prisons in Washington State and Kansas. They threw tear-gas canisters into the cell house. They fired machine guns and mortars. Marines were called in to guard the prisoners who were still in the Yard, locked outside the cell house. Coast Guard boats circled the island.

Eventually, a hole was drilled into the cell-house ceiling, and grenades and explosives were dropped through. The blasts could be heard across the bay in San Francisco, where people watched through binoculars as the battle raged.

At the end of the Battle of Alcatraz, Coy, Cretzer, and Hubbard were found dead. "Crazy Sam" Shockley and another partner in crime were put on trial and convicted. They were executed in the gas chamber at San Quentin State Prison, seated next to each other. The sixth man received an additional ninety-nine-year sentence. Officer Miller died from his injuries. Remarkably, the other hostages survived. But another guard, Harold Stites, was killed in the battle.

The Battle of Alcatraz was not the first escape attempt at Alcatraz. And it wouldn't be the last. In its twenty-nine years as a federal prison, Alcatraz saw fourteen escape attempts. No one escaped alive . . . but not everyone believes that.

Perhaps the most famous attempt was the thirteenth, in June 1962. Frank Lee Morris, a genius and an escape artist, planned an escape with three partners: Allen Clayton West, and brothers John and Clarence Anglin.

Frank Lee Morris   Allen Clayton West   Clarence Anglin   John Anglin

Over many months, every night, the men chipped away at the wall surrounding their ventilator grilles. They used spoons stolen from the Mess Hall. They wanted to reach a corridor on the other side. Out of view from the guards, this corridor ran between the two rows of cells in the block.

Bit by bit, the wall around the ventilator grilles crumbled. The rocks and dust were flushed down the toilet or scattered the next day when they went to work. While two men dug, the others acted as lookouts. To cover the holes they were digging, they made a look-alike grille out of cardboard. They painted the grille to match the real thing perfectly.

Part two of the plan involved more arts and crafts! Using soap, cotton rags, toilet paper, and real hair collected from the barbershop, they built papier-mâché heads, then painted them. These heads would be placed on their beds the night of the escape, to fool the guard who made the nighttime counts.

Finally, they needed a way off the island. Frank Morris got an idea from *Popular Mechanics* magazine. He would create a raft and life vests out of raincoats.

After lights-out on June 11, Morris and the Anglin brothers put their dummy heads to bed, then squeezed out of their cells into the corridor. Allen West couldn't remove the grille from his cell wall in time. It was stuck. He was left behind.

Morris and the Anglins climbed up to the roof
of the building. Avoiding the spotlights from the
watchtowers, they climbed down a fifty-foot shaft
to the ground and ran toward the water. After
scaling a barbed-wire fence, they finally reached
the waters of San Francisco Bay. They inflated
their raft, then got in the water and started
paddling to shore.

The next morning, a guard tried to wake up Frank Morris. When he nudged Morris's "head," it rolled onto the floor. That must have been a surprise!

Alcatraz went on lockdown right away. The Federal Bureau of Investigation (FBI) arrived with bloodhounds. They followed the inmates' trail to

the water. State and local police joined the Coast Guard in the biggest manhunt in San Francisco history.

Pieces of the raft and life vests were found scattered across the Bay Area. But no suspicious crimes—no robberies, no stolen cars—were reported nearby. The men seemed to have vanished into thin air.

The FBI closed the case in 1979. Frank Morris and the Anglins were declared dead. Drowned in the churning waters of San Francisco Bay.

But no bodies have ever been found.

CHAPTER 6
This Rock Is Ours

Frank Morris's famous escape revealed something that many already suspected: Alcatraz was falling apart. The salty air had damaged the concrete. The cell house wouldn't be safe during an earthquake. The Rock was due for some very pricey repairs.

And running Alcatraz was expensive enough already! All supplies had to be brought in by boat. It cost the government three times more money to keep an inmate at Alcatraz than at US Penitentiary Atlanta.

In the autumn of 1962, prisoners at Alcatraz started getting moved to other federal prisons. On March 21, 1963, the final twenty-seven prisoners left after lunch, which lasted exactly twenty

minutes. Warden Olin G. Blackwell kept things on schedule to the very last day.

The warden invited members of the press to cover the event. It was the first time since the Battle of Alcatraz, sixteen years earlier, that outsiders had been allowed inside the prison.

As the last prisoner left the island, a reporter asked him how he felt. "Alcatraz was never no good for nobody," he said.

The mayor of San Francisco asked for ideas for what to do with Alcatraz, now that the prison was closed for good. The people of San Francisco had never liked the gloomy prison in their backyard. Many wrote to the mayor.

One idea was to build a Statue of Justice, to match the Statue of Liberty on the East Coast. Another was to turn Alcatraz into a casino! A rich oil tycoon from Texas wanted to build a theme park and shopping center, complete with restaurants and a 364-foot-tall "Space Tower"!

Proposed "Space Tower"

While people argued about what to do with The Rock, a group of Native Americans calling themselves the Indians of All Tribes claimed that Alcatraz belonged to them. They were led by a college student named Richard Oakes, who said that a treaty signed by the US government in 1868 gave them ownership of Alcatraz.

Richard Oakes

The Indians of All Tribes wanted to occupy Alcatraz to raise awareness of how their people had been treated for so long.

As early as the 1890s, Hopi Indians had been imprisoned at Alcatraz. Their crime was refusing to send their children to government schools, which were often very far away from home.

In 1953, the US government passed a law to begin closing reservations, the lands where Native Americans lived. More than one hundred thousand Native Americans were moved against their will—sent away to live in big cities, like San Francisco.

Native Americans were losing their way of life.

On November 20, 1969, the Indians of All Tribes arrived on Alcatraz. Soon, a hundred people lived on the island. At times there were as many as *four* hundred!

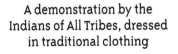

A demonstration by the Indians of All Tribes, dressed in traditional clothing

For a year and a half, they lived on Alcatraz. They made plans for a Native American university. They wanted to tear down existing buildings and replace them with a large roundhouse made of steel, glass, and redwood. They published a newsletter. Supporters sent them supplies. A teepee was erected. Fires for cooking food burned in the Yard.

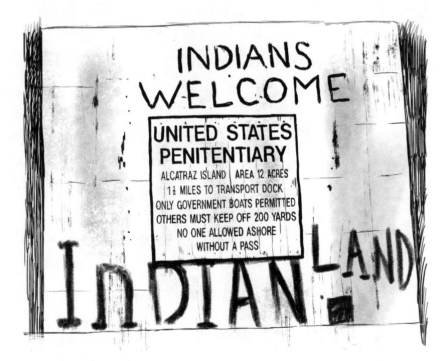

Even though the protesters were eventually removed from the island, their actions inspired others. Evidence of their time on The Rock remains to this day.

After the occupation of Alcatraz, the US government changed its policy toward the Native Americans. They recognized the tribes' right to self-rule. In a strange way, going to the island prison helped free Native Americans to decide their futures for themselves.

CHAPTER 7
Alcatraz Now

In 1972, Alcatraz became part of the Golden Gate National Recreation Area. The next year, it opened to the public as a national park. It's been a popular tourist spot ever since.

But it's not just people who come here. The
Rock is the perfect nesting ground for many
types of seabirds. They build nests in the rubble
that remains of the warden's mansion and other
buildings. They hunt for fish in the tide pools.
California slender salamanders and banana slugs
live among the ruins, too.

Human visitors arrive 362 days a year. They come by boat and follow in the footsteps of 1,545 federal prisoners before them. After a long uphill walk to the prison basement, they are given headphones. They choose from eleven different languages and take an audio tour of the grounds. The English-language tour is narrated by former guards and inmates. Now visitors can learn the truth behind the Hollywood myths.

Alcatraz in the Movies

Birdman of Alcatraz (1962) was nominated for four Academy Awards and considered a great film. However, it was inaccurate in its portrayal of the real-life Robert Stroud. (For example, Stroud's birds weren't even allowed on Alcatraz!)

Escape from Alcatraz (1979) starred Clint Eastwood as Frank Morris. It was about the daring 1962 escape and was mostly true to life.

Murder in the First (1995) starred Kevin Bacon and Christian Slater. It told the story of Henri Young, a man who claimed in court that Alcatraz's cruel punishments led him to murder a fellow inmate. The movie was not very accurate.

The Rock (1996) and part of *X-Men: The Last Stand* (2006) were also set on Alcatraz.

On the tour of Alcatraz, people enter the dreaded Cell 14-D. They stand in the Strip Cell and try to imagine what it felt like to be there in the dark, cold and hungry and alone. They

see chips in the concrete floor, where grenades exploded during the Battle of Alcatraz. They peek down the corridor Frank Morris and the Anglin brothers tunneled to.

At the height of Prohibition in 1930, about one out of every 650 Americans was in jail or prison. In 2008, it had risen to one out of a hundred. Violent crime has actually *fallen* since the bloody days of Gangland, but today people are thrown into prison for more reasons than in those years.

As thrilling as the legends of Alcatraz are, it is important to think about what life on The Rock was like. At times it was horrible. But it could also be helpful. Warden Johnston believed that structure and training could prepare inmates for life after prison. A better life. Not every warden thinks the same way today. With more Americans in prison than ever before, lessons and methods from the past can be valuable.

For now, Alcatraz, the Island of the Pelicans, has returned to the birds. But The Rock will always remain a stark and fascinating reminder of our past.

Timeline of Alcatraz and San Francisco

c. 8000 BC	Native Americans visit Alcatraz Island to fish and collect eggs from seabird nests
AD 1542	Spanish explorers begin to map the northern California coast
1775	Juan Manuel de Ayala of Spain becomes the first known European to see Alcatraz Island
1776	Spanish colonists found San Francisco
1848	California becomes part of the United States
1849	Gold Rush brings prospectors west; San Francisco's population explodes
1859	Fort Alcatraz opens
1861	US Civil War begins; first military prisoners arrive on The Rock
1895	Hopi Indians imprisoned at Alcatraz
1906	Earthquake devastates the area; Alcatraz temporarily houses prisoners from the city's jails
1934	The US Department of Justice takes over Alcatraz
	Al Capone arrives at Alcatraz on August 22
1946	The Battle of Alcatraz rages from May 2 to 4
1962	Three prisoners break out of Alcatraz and are never found
1963	Alcatraz's last prisoners leave the island on March 21
1969–1971	The Indians of All Tribes occupy Alcatraz Island for a year and a half
1973	Alcatraz becomes a national park, open to the public

Timeline of the World

c. 8000 BC	Cats move into human settlements and become pets
AD 1508–1512	In Rome, Michelangelo paints the Sistine Chapel's ceiling
1775	Jane Austen, author of *Pride and Prejudice*, is born in England
1776	The United States of America declares its independence from Great Britain
1821	Mexico wins its independence from Spain
1845	Florida becomes the twenty-seventh state in the Union
1851	The foot-powered sewing machine is invented
1859	Charles Darwin publishes his theory of evolution in the book *On the Origin of Species*
1866	Permanent telegraph cables cross the Atlantic, allowing almost instant communication between the United States and Europe
1867	Alfred Nobel of Sweden invents dynamite
1896	First modern Olympic Games are held in Athens, Greece
1903	First World Series is played between Boston and Pittsburgh
1905	First modern movie theater in the United States opens in Pittsburgh
1932	Amelia Earhart becomes the first woman to fly solo across the Atlantic
1945	World War II ends; the United Nations is founded
1963	President John F. Kennedy is assassinated
1969	*Sesame Street* airs for the first time
1973	Sears Tower opens in Chicago and remains the world's tallest building until 1998

Bibliography

Alcatraz: The Final Sentence. Huckleberry Films, 1988. DVD.

Campbell, Eileen, Michael Rigsby, and Tacy Dunham. *Discover Alcatraz: A Tour of the Rock.* San Francisco: Golden Gate National Parks Conservancy, 1996.

Esslinger, Michael. *Alcatraz: A Definitive History of the Penitentiary Years.* Carmel, CA: Ocean View Publishing, 2003.

Fritscher, Lisa. "History of Alcatraz Island." *USA Today Online.* http://traveltips.usatoday.com/history-alcatraz-island-11753.html.

History.com Staff. "Al Capone." A&E Networks, 2009. http://www.history.com/topics/al-capone.

Lapin, Nicole, and Jason Hanna. "1969 Alcatraz takeover 'changed the whole course of history.'" CNN.com. November 20, 2009. http://www.cnn.com/2009/CRIME/11/20/alcatraz.indian.occupation/.

Lieber, Robert (ed). *Dining In: USP Alcatraz Food Magazine.* San Francisco: Golden Gate National Parks Conservancy, 2008.

Wellman, Gregory L. *A History of Alcatraz Island 1853–2008.* Charleston, SC: Arcadia Publishing, 2008.

MARIN
COUNTY

HORSESHOE
BAY

SAN FRANCISCO
BAY

GOLDEN GATE
BRIDGE

PRESIDIO

SAN
FRANCISCO

LINCOLN BLVD.

VETERANS BLVD.

SHERIDAN AVE.

LINCOLN BLVD.

PRESIDIO BLVD.

PRESIDIO
HEIGHTS